Realizing your dream of full time RV travel

By Krista Madlung

Realizing your dream of full time RV travel
All rights reserved
February 2, 2021
Copyright@2021 Wild Daisy Productions
Wilddaisyproductions.com@gmail.com
ISBN: 9798595144698

No part of this book may be reproduced or transmitted in any form or by any means, electronic or mechanical, including photocopying, recording or by any information storage and retrieval system, without the permission in writing from Wild Daisy Productions.

Contents

Introduction	**1**
Chapter One	**7**
Where to begin	*7*
Title of your plan	*9*
Leave date	*10*
Duration	*10*
Goals	*11*
Chapter Two	**13**
Need's List	*13*
Travel Style	*14*
Stuff	*21*
Chapter Three	**27**
Budget...money, money, money	*27*
Chapter Four	**33**
Working from the road	*33*
Chapter Five	**37**
Assets – House, Land, Vehicle, Boat	*37*
Chapter Six	**39**
The rest of your belongings	*39*
Chapter Seven	**43**
Planning your route...or wander aimlessly	*43*

Chapter Eight   **49**

Protection of life and property   *49*

Chapter Nine   **53**

Mail   *53*

Important papers   *54*

Will or power of attorney   *55*

Chapter Ten   **57**

Rodents and bugs   *57*

Wild animals   *58*

Chapter Eleven   **61**

Significant other   *61*

Family or Friends   *62*

Children   *62*

Chapter Twelve   **65**

Pets   *65*

Chapter Thirteen   **73**

Emotionally and psychologically prepared   *73*

Sample Plan   **77**

About the author   **85**

Introduction

Have you ever thought about selling everything you own, moving into an RV and traveling the country?

Do people in your life ask if you are crazy?

Do they also ask what you will do for money, how will you eat, how will you live, what if all your stuff gets stolen, and the best question of all, what if you are murdered??

I have answers!!!! Tell them that you will plan, save, budget, take safety precautions and have insurance in case your property is stolen...and that you won't care if you are murdered, because you'll be dead.

And did you notice that all of those questions are surrounded by fear.

Fear of the unknown.

Well guess what, buttercup...life is all about the unknown. You don't know what will happen in your future. You could die right now...reading this book.

My philosophy is that when death comes for you there is nothing you can do about it, so why worry.

I remember hearing about a guy who was sleeping in his house, in his bedroom, in his bed when a huge sinkhole opened up underneath him and he was gone, into the abyss...presumed dead, never to be heard from again. Scary stuff!

So why not do what you want, within reason, and the law of course, until death decides it is your time to go?

For me, I have wanted to do this traveling thing for a long time, so I said to myself: why not go before I get too old to enjoy it?

Growing up, I would watch slideshows of my grandparents (on my dad's side) on cross country camping trips with their trailer. My grandparents, and a few of their relatives and friends, all towing their trailers, traveling around the good ole US of A.

As a child, I was lucky enough to go on numerous camping trips with them...within our state only, of course.

My grandparents would load up the truck and trailer with everything we needed for a few days or sometimes up to a week. My grandpa would drive like crazy to the other side of the state so we could camp where it was warm and dry.

My cousins would also go with their grandparents. Our extended family would have multiple campsites throughout the campground.

One of my favorite memories was of my grandpa making silver dollar sized beer pancakes. Yes, he used beer and water to mix into the pancake batter. (People who know me would affectionately say that this explains a lot...beer in my food).

My cousins and I would have a contest every morning to see who could eat the most pancakes. We took turns winning!

My parents and I still make beer pancakes...it's a family tradition.

My grandma on my mom's side always talked about traveling. She wanted to buy a motorhome and travel the country. My grandparents got as far as retiring and buying the motorhome. They took a couple of short trips within the state until my grandma's Parkinson's disease got too bad, and my grandpa's emphysema got so bad he had to be hooked to oxygen full time. That was crushing. They had to sell the motorhome and my grandma had to come to terms with not fulfilling her dream of traveling.

Both sets of grandparents have since passed away, but I have such amazing and valuable memories of each of them. I was truly blessed to have had as much time as I did with all of them.

My family moved to Alaska during my 6th, 7th and 8th grade school years. That was quite a unique experience. Not many people can say they spent three years in two different logging camps.

But other than the three years in Alaska, I have spent the better part of my life in the same county that I was born in. Not that I am complaining...too much. But I have always wanted to see the world.

I just felt that I needed to stay home and help to take care of my ailing grandparents, cousins and others in my life...whether they needed it or not.

Then I met a guy, got pregnant and then married (yes in that order...don't judge) and I didn't want to be traveling with a child. I wanted him to have some roots, like I did. Plus, I don't think either of my son's grandparents or extended family would have been too happy with me if I took him away from them and traveled around the country in an RV. He was very spoiled, as it should be, and I wanted him to have a strong relationship with his grandparents, like I did with mine.

Looking back now, though, I should have taken him on extended trips every summer so he could have had more experiences traveling. But I can't change it now.

At the time of my divorce, my son was in the sixth grade. With just one child, and not able to have any more, I was going to be an empty nester in less than seven years. I figured when he headed off to college I could head off on my travels!!

Two years after my divorce I was finally ready to write my travel plan...my five-year plan.

When I first started writing the plan, I had wanted to travel outside of the USA. Australia, Italy, New Zealand, Europe...everywhere that Americans were liked. But the more I dove into the plan, the more abundantly clear it was to me that I first needed to see my own country because I had not visited many places in the USA.

I revised the plan and wrote down how I was going to use the next five years to get prepared to live fulltime in an RV and travel the country.

That was in 2011...remember that plans are fluid and always able to be updated.

I continued to update my plan all the way up until I actually pulled the trigger and left town in my truck with my trailer in tow...in 2020.

Yes, the weirdest year in history – 2020, I decided to make the leap. In my defense I actually decided in December of 2019 that I would leave the following year.

How did I come up with an exact day to leave?

I turned the big 5-0 on August 30th, 2020, so what better present to myself than to leave on September 1st.

I figured I needed the 31st to recover from my hopefully epic 50th birthday party!

What I didn't know was that 2020 was going to be epic...pandemic!

A lot of people in my life kept asking me if I was still going to be leaving with all that was going on in the world; lockdowns, riots, and of course, the pandemic.

I answered, what better time to do this than right now! Especially if the world as we know it was ending.

And once I pulled the pin on my decision to leave, I couldn't put that pin back in.

So how did I do it? What was in my plan?

I had done extensive research over the last 10 years of what it would look like once I was on the road, but I actually didn't find much information about how to plan to do it.

And now, since I've been on the road, I keep getting the same questions about how I did this. How did I realize my dream?

You can find printable worksheets to assist you with developing your plan in the back of this book.

This book will also cover all of the sections of the plan with tips and questions you might need to answer in order to develop your plan.

So, that's what I'm going to write about in this book: how to start, what you will need to think about, what decisions you will need to make and what to expect when you actually drive away in your RV on your great adventure!

Let's do this!!!!!!

6

Chapter One

Where to begin

When I started putting together my plan in 2011, I didn't realize how much I had not thought of. I needed to add a lot more to my to-do list before embarking on my adventure.

To get started, I listed a few things that needed to be completed prior to me leaving.

- Sell my home
- Get rid of most personal possessions
- Reduce the amount of pets
- Save money
- Buy a new car
- Only have one job

That's all that I had written down...boy was I naïve.

Yes, those initial items would probably be beneficial, but I had no idea how much more was going to go into the plan.

I also didn't know how my life would change over the next eight years, and where I would end up after the whirlwind of life picked me up and dropped me on my head!

Before we get into the plan of it all, there are some key ingredients for making your dream work.

My village

I am very thankful for my large support system, especially my parents.

My dad went through my whole trailer, wire by wire, to make sure that it was in working order. He installed a new axle, made sure the floor and walls were safe and helped me make sure all the systems were up and running.

My mom painted the interior, found a new mattress for the bed, sewed the cushion covers and made all the curtains. She also bought me a spare tire cover, put together a sewing kit and a clothesline kit.

They both also bought me many items for the trailer as birthday and Christmas gifts.

Other family and friends also helped me get ready, whether by installing trailer brakes in my truck, helping to primer the inside of the trailer or helping me sell all of my belongings at a garage sale.

Talk with family and friends about what your dreams are...they may be able to help you achieve it!

Research, research, research.

You must do your research. I did over ten years of research before I left. You will need to know things that you never in your life thought you would need to know.

There is so much more information out there on social media than when I first thought about full time traveling. Take advantage of it.

Ok, let's begin talking about the plan!

First and foremost, the biggest takeaway I can offer you is:

"Please do not type up your plan and then never look at it again".

Out of sight, out of mind. If you are not routinely reviewing and updating your plan, then your dream may die. I do not want that for you. So, please, have that plan available and in view!

I had a current copy of my plan printed out at all times and when I was feeling inspired or wanting to focus on my dream, I would get it off my book shelf, review it, use a red pen to make changes, and then update and reprint it on my laptop.

I would replace the old plan with the updated one in a three-ring binder, and with a smile, placed it back up on that book shelf. It was satisfying knowing that I was one day closer to my dream. You have no idea what a stress reliever that was for me!

Title of your plan

The title of my plan changed every year, obviously, since it was a countdown of years. (my five-year plan is pretty specific)

Once you name your plan, talk about it with your family and friends...even strangers you meet on the street! This will ensure that your dream is being put out into the universe and will feel closer to reality.

Most of the people in my life knew exactly what I was talking about when I mentioned "my five-year plan".

It made it even more real for me when family and friends brought my plan up in normal conversations. It made my dream come alive; it was going to come true. My plan was going to be executed!

Leave date

One way to make this dream a reality is to decide on a leave date. If that date is fast approaching and you don't feel prepared enough or your situation has changed so that you aren't able to leave, then push that date back. It's ok. Don't beat yourself up about it.
My original leave date was in September of 2016. It's ok if you are not ready, don't force yourself to stick with a date. I would rather see you prepared before hitting the road.
But don't keep pushing that date back either. Being scared is not a reason to keep moving that leave date. Remember that all of your fears are lies, especially if you are prepared!
Did I feel 100% ready to leave town when I did? To be honest, no. I felt I had more things to get done, but guess what, I found out that I was prepared, and I was ready to face those fears.
And boy am I glad I did! It has been well worth it!

Duration

This is where you will decide how long you will be on the road traveling.
Will it be forever?
Will it be for one year, two years, five years?
Will it be until you have fulfilled your goals?
Will it be until you run out of money?
I have always planned to travel for at least one year. I want to travel and see everything I want within that first year and give my writing career time to develop.

But I'm also leaving the option open for a longer period of time.

When trying to figure out your duration, realize that your timeline may extend over certain holidays that you typically spend with family and friends.

Will you go home for those holidays?

Will your family and friends join you on the road for the holidays?

For me, I have opted to stay on the road. Experiencing the holidays in other parts of the country is so intriguing for me!

Having this conversation beforehand with family and friends may be beneficial. It may soften the blow of this news to those that counted on you being there for the holidays.

If you have children traveling with you, make sure to talk with them about the holiday plans prior to the day before.

If you decide to stay on the road instead of going to grandma's house for Christmas, tell them you will be starting a new tradition and make it fun for them.

Recently it was my nephew's birthday. He is an adult, but birthdays are huge in our family. He decided to have a video chat birthday party where we dressed up, had a drink of our choice in our hands to toast him turning a year older. It's a great way to stay connected to those you love.

Goals

Write down the goals you wish to achieve. The goals that are currently listed in my plan are as follows:

- To visit all the places on my bucket list in the USA within a year.
- To continue to write a blog and to finish writing my books and screenplay that I have already started.
- To also write and illustrate children's books of my pets' traveling adventures.
- To slow down and really enjoy the present.
- Follow the sun.

I continue to add to my goals, even though I'm already on the road. Sometimes daily.

For instance, I have been told that I should be taking videos of my travel adventures to upload onto my YouTube channel. Not something that was on my radar when I began writing my plan.

Writing this book was not on my radar either, but here it is!

Another reason for writing down your goals is because when things get tough on the road, and they will, or when you feel like giving up before you even start, I want you to re-read those goals. Use them to inspire you, to encourage you to keep going. Like a pep talk to yourself...a goal-oriented pep talk.

Now that we have a plan name, leave date, duration of your adventure and your goals, let's put that plan together!

Chapter Two

Need's List

One major section in your plan will be a need's list; what will you need to purchase or acquire prior to your leave date.

Some of the items I listed in my plan are shown below:

Need	Cost	Notes	Date Acquired
Travel Trailer	Free		Sept 2017
Truck to pull trailer	$3,300		Feb 2019
Cover for truck bed	Berry pie		Aug 2020
Camping Chairs	$70		May 2020
Trailer Battery	$120		Aug 2020
Propane Tanks	Birthday Present		June 2020
Kitchen Items	$100		Aug 2020
Cat cage	$70		June 2020
Air Conditioner	$300		May 2020
New Hitch	$200		Aug 2020
Cooler	$60		May 2020
Bathroom kit	$30		June 2020
Pet kit for truck	$20		Jan 2020
Blog / website	$100	Per year	Feb 2016

This is not the full list, but you can see the types of items I needed to begin. It was nice to check off items as I was able to obtain them. This made me feel very accomplished and it kept my eye on the prize as far as saving money, and holding myself to my leave date.

This list was always changing. All the way up until the day I left.

First on the list is what you will be traveling in and what your travel style will be.

Travel Style

I was very fortunate to have received, for free, a 1967 Bell Camping Trailer. Again, for free.

About four years ago my wonderful friends did not want the trailer taking up space in their barn anymore, so they signed it over to me.

My other wonderful friends stored it in their shop for a few years before I was able to start working on it.

I do realize that not everyone has this scenario happen to them. But all of my friends had known about my five-year plan, so they happily reached out to help me begin to achieve my dream! Again, takes a village!

Because of this pandemic year trailers can be extremely expensive, even used or un-road-worthy ones.

Before I started on this adventure, multiple people asked if I would sell them my trailer. I was even offered $15,000 for my upgraded trailer. My dad said I should have taken it.

Nope. My dream is worth more than $15,000...a lot more.

Let's discuss your style.

What you need to decide is what type of traveling mode will it require to obtain your goals.
Will it be with a trailer, or a motorhome, or a van, or a converted school bus, or...the possibilities are endless.
Read each of your goals to determine what it will take.
Some examples are listed below along with at least one pro and one con for each:

Truck with trailer
Pro's: you are able to disconnect your trailer and utilize your vehicle for sight-seeing or running errands
Con's: you are unable to get to off-road remote areas or you could damage or put major wear and tear on your trailer by trying to access some areas

Truck with a fifth wheel trailer
Pro's: you are able to disconnect your trailer and utilize your vehicle for sight-seeing or running errands
Con's: in order to tow a fifth-wheel trailer you will need to give up the space in the bed of your truck for the special hitch

Truck with a pop-up trailer
Pro's: you are able to disconnect your trailer and utilize your vehicle for sight-seeing or running errands
Con's: these types of trailers don't do well in cold or rainy weather and they are easy to break into

Truck with a teardrop trailer
Pro's: you are able to disconnect your trailer and utilize your vehicle for sight-seeing or running errands
Con's: there is only room for sleeping quarters, no bathroom and only some models have a kitchen on the outside of the trailer

Truck with a toy hauler
Pro's: you are able to disconnect your trailer and utilize your vehicle for sight-seeing or running errands
Con's: these trailers are longer than most and the types of camping will be restricted to larger campsites

Truck with camper
Pro's: Fuel costs will be lower than if you are towing a trailer or driving a motorhome
Con's: truck and living space all in one, would have to take off camper in order to utilize truck for errands. Would need to break camp in order to run errands

Motorhome
Pro's: more space and comfort while driving for multiple travelers and pets
Con's: would need to break camp in order to sight see or run errands

Motorhome towing a car
Pro's: more space and comfort while driving for multiple travelers and pets
Con's: gas milage will increase considerably, and you will need a large campsite

Remodeled school bus
Pro's: more space and comfort while driving for multiple travelers and pets
Con's: would need to break camp in order to sight see or run errands

Remodeled horse trailer
Pro's: you are able to disconnect your trailer and utilize your vehicle for sight-seeing or running errands

Con's: you are unable to get to off-road remote areas or you could damage or put major wear and tear on your trailer by trying to access some areas

Remodeled box van
Pro's: more space and comfort while driving for multiple travelers and pets
Con's: would need to break camp in order to sight see or run errands

Van
Pro's: you are able to go to off road and remote areas
Con's: limited or no space to sleep, shower or cook, it would be expensive to stay in motels and eat out during your trip

Car or truck
Pro's: you are able to go off-road and to remote areas; gas milage would be the most inexpensive of all the choices
Con's: limited or no space to sleep, shower or cook, it would be expensive to stay in motels throughout your trip

There are so many options out there, but in order to decide on your travel style you will need to decide which of the con's you can live with.
Feel free to also add to this list in order to figure out which travel style to choose.
One of the reasons I wanted a truck and trailer combo is because I wanted to have a vehicle while out on the road. But just one vehicle.
The gas for a motorhome was more than I could afford, and if it broke down and was in the shop for repairs, where would I live until it was fixed?

Plus I wanted to be able to boondock (the practice of pulling off the highway to stay at free locations in spots that have zero or limited facilities), and not having to rely on services at a campground and still live in the trailer.

I also knew I wanted something small, and something without tip outs. As my dad says, tip outs are just one more thing that could break that I would eventually have to fix.

Still need help figuring out what your style will be?

I suggest that you take tours of multiple types of trailers, or motorhomes. Or think outside the box to learn about what you can convert into a mobile, but livable, space.

One thing I have heard over and over from other full time RV'ers I meet on the road is that they wish that they would have gotten a smaller RV.

When coming from a large house it is sometimes a shock to the system to move into a small RV. But you truly do not need as much space as you think you will. Especially if you are following warm weather where you can utilize the outdoors as livable space.

I also suggest taking the trailer, or motorhome or whatever you decide upon, out for test trips...numerous test trips.

One thing you will find out, whatever you decide to take with you on your adventure, is that they will all break down...some more than others.

RV'ers that I have talked to think that my 1967 Bell trailer will last a lot longer than their 2020 motorhome, or 2018 trailer. Sad, but true, these things break, and if one of your goals is to move locations often, that will cause a lot of wear and tear on your motorhome or trailer.

If your goal is to stay in just a couple of different places for long periods of time, then maybe a larger trailer or motorhome with all the bells and whistles is for you. If I were to live in one RV park for most or all the year, I would purchase a much larger trailer. Maybe even with tip outs...don't tell my dad.

There are a lot of people traveling in vans nowadays. That would cut your costs down considerably. But, some things to think about before you choose this path is where will you go to the bathroom, where will you shower, and most importantly, if you are chasing the sun during your travels, how will you get a/c to work without running your van all night? I know that some of the newer vans can plug into shore power at campgrounds, but is your van equipped to do that or will you have to modify it?

A solution to having a second mode of transportation could be to have bicycles, electric bikes or scooters.

I have camped beside many travelers in their vans who have bikes that they use to ride into town. Electric bikes can help you go a longer distance without any real effort.

I would love to travel around Alaska at some point in my life, but my trailer would never make it in the Alaska weather or terrain. Buying and adapting a small van would be my choice for that type of terrain.

My trailer bounces way too much and things break inside if I go down a rough road, or even a rough highway. So currently I'm more of a smooth road type of traveler. And to say that my trailer is insulated is a lie. The walls are literally the inside paneling with the outer metal siding...the insulation has since fallen to the bottom of the wall or has been carried away by mice.

If you do decide to buy a trailer, what will you tow it with?

The same friend that I received the trailer from contacted me last year and told me his son was selling his truck, and it would be perfect to tow my trailer. Sold!

The truck is solid. It's a 1995 GMC Sierra.

I decided on an older truck because I believe it is easier to work on, and cheaper to fix. Plus, I didn't need anything too big to tow my very light, very small trailer.

The truck needed some fixes prior to me hitting the road. It needed a new radiator, and the air conditioning needed to be fixed and filled.

I also needed something to cover the bed of the truck with. Something that locked.

My small trailer does not have much storage, so I needed the bed of my truck to store things like water, and other supplies. A family friend had a bed cover that fit my truck perfectly. All he wanted was a berry pie from my mom...sold!

It may seem like I have been lucky getting things for free or low cost. But like I will continue to say in this book, everyone knew what my dream was and over the years when one of my family or friends came upon something that they thought would help me achieve that dream they didn't hesitate to call me. And I was always appreciative!

Keep in mind that when you receive free items, you may still need to put money into getting them to where you need them.

My trailer needed some work, like a new axle and new tires. My truck has also needed some work, and most of that was done after I left town.

With free items you are also unable to choose the color of them. Nothing I have matches; my trailer is blue and white, my truck is maroon, and the truck bed cover is a faded blue...red white and blue coming down the road.

I told my mom I wanted to appear like a ragamuffin, that way maybe people wouldn't think I had anything worth stealing!

The mismatch of it all doesn't bother me. I'm used to hand-me-down's. But for some people they want things to match, or to be much newer. That is all up to you, it's your style, remember!

Before settling on a traveling style decide if you will be living on the road alone.

If not, who will be going with you?

• Significant other?
• Partner?
• Family member?
• Friend?
• Children?
• Pets?

What are their needs?

I am mainly traveling alone, with my dog and two cats, so having a small 14' trailer is perfect for my goals!

My boyfriend and friends may come travel for a while with me, so I will have to be able to accommodate them in my trailer.

If you are traveling with children then you may consider a larger living space.

I go into more detail about traveling alone, with someone, with children and with pets in Chapter Eleven and Twelve.

Stuff

With any choice you make regarding your travel style you will need to 'furnish' that space.

On the needs list I had numerous items that were required in order to make my travel style work for me; some of those items I didn't even realize I needed until I started traveling.

If I would have experienced more trips with my trailer before my leave date, I may have been a little more prepared than I actually was.

One item I had debated over before I started traveling was a generator. I wasn't sure if I wanted one. I thought that my trailer battery would be sufficient enough to run the trailer.

I was very wrong.

I was not thinking about my electric cooler or my electric air conditioning unit.

During the first month of being on the road I stayed at two campgrounds that did not have shore power to connect to...during one such stay I found myself quickly buying a generator.

On a positive note, I found it cheaper in California then when I was pricing them at home in Washington State.

It was nice to have the option of a generator for my trailer. In talking with other full time RV'ers with bigger and newer trailers or motorhomes, they said a generator was the first thing they bought.

This is something you will need to figure out for yourself. Decide if there will be any time you may not have access to shore power. Because not having anywhere to plug in my air conditioning unit in hot weather was not fun. Nor was it fun to have run my trailer battery down so far that it refused to charge anymore. Luckily it was under warranty so it was replaced for free!

My older trailer does not have the fancy pull down awnings like most of the newer trailers or motorhomes have. But my dad still had my grandparent's awning from their old trailer from the 60's.

22

My dad watched YouTube videos on how to make tent poles out of PVC pipe, and my mom put grommets on the canvas awning so I could use carabiner's to attach it to the hooks on my trailer roof.

At some campgrounds I am unable to put stakes into the ground to put up my awning. Or if it's too windy, the awning won't work.

On the road I purchased an inexpensive stand- alone canopy to use when I can't put stakes in the ground. And for the wind issue, I just keep things buttoned up until the wind stops.

Air conditioning units were not built into my vintage trailer. Back then it was a fan and a block of ice...that was air conditioning at its finest.

Because of this fact, I researched and bought a portable unit on wheels. I just had to figure out how to vent it.

My first thought was to hang the hose out one of the windows, but upon traveling, I had to come up with another solution. Especially since I couldn't leave the window wide open because my cats and possibly my dog would jump out!

In retrospect I found out that I missed having my dad help me and to have his shop with all those tools to use.

But I figured it out after a few weeks on my own, and installed a port on one of my windows. Velcro, glue and a dowel to lock the window in place...McGyver style.

I wished I knew that this was something I would have needed to get setup prior to hitting the road. That's why heading out on more than one practice trip is so necessary.

Most of the items you will need can come from things you already have in your house.

I was able to utilize a lot of items that I already owned, which saved me loads of money.

Some of those items were:

- Kitchen items

- Bathroom items
- Toiletries
- Laundry items
- Tools and a tool box
- Auto tools and maintenance items (oil, antifreeze)
- Bedding including pillows
- Pet supplies
- Camping chairs
- Food
- Décor (pictures, plants, lighting)
- Rugs
- Curtains
- Storage boxes, bins, baskets
- Laptop and printer
- Hooks for hanging items
- Camping gear

For me, I had a lot of these items, but some things were too large for my small trailer kitchen. Such as my cooking pans. My stove burners are very small, so I purchased smaller pans at a discount store.

I also decided that I wanted silverware that matched my trailer, and a countertop ice maker. It's sometimes the little things that make me smile, like the new can opener I bought that matches my stove.

In order for me to purchase those new items I had to justify them. The can opener was a no brainer. I had been using the same can opener for ten years. So purchasing one that actually opened a can in one turn around instead of three turns was a selling point. The silverware and ice maker I found on sale, plus my old silverware went to my ex roommate who needed it. Justification...

Other items I needed to purchase were a laundry basket, a dishwashing tub and a dish drying rack. And all of them had to be small or able to fold flat. That was a must have for me and my small space.

It's ok to purchase all new items, just make sure that it's within your budget. I would hate to see you spend all of your travel budget on stuff instead of your dream!

While in my rental home, I loved shopping at a bulk store. So, in my bathroom closet I had a lot of Q-tips, shampoo, toothpaste and body soap. And I mean a lot!

I estimated how long it would take me to use each of those items and then chose accordingly what would go into my bathroom basket in my trailer. The rest I gave away to friends and family.

I did the same with my laundry items; soap and dryer sheets. I also collected quarters for about a year to use on the road to do laundry, and in some campgrounds, to pay for hot showers. Plus, my mom gifted me a jar of quarters for my birthday!

I purchased a bathroom organizer with a hanging hook. I utilize campground showers and it's so nice to be able to take one bag with all the items I need to take a shower and get ready for the day, or night.

Once you figured out what you will be traveling in and what items you will need to purchase, add those to your needs list.

If you are a person who is being asked what you want for your birthday or for Christmas, hand someone your needs list or send them a link for the item you'd like them to gift you.

The gift giver will be happy to have helped you on the road to your dream, and you will be saving money in the process.

Chapter Three

Budget...money, money, money

This is the biggest question I get...what are you going to do for money?

I also get comments like, 'you must be rich!' or 'are your parents paying for this trip?'...nope.

First...I'm not even close to being rich. Second, although my parents helped me with the trailer and paid for some of the upgrades in lieu of birthday and Christmas gifts, which was so unbelievably awesome of them, I have saved my own money to do this.

I also sold many of my belongings to help pay for the upgrades to the trailer and items to furnish it with. I also have been collecting items for years from family, friends, garage sales and even free on the side of the road events.

While doing my research for my adventure, I purchased a book called Vagabonding by Rolf Potts.

He mainly talks about traveling overseas, but some of those same statements he makes also applies to the USA. A great book to read if you are considering this type of adventure or life style.

This was a very motivating book for me. It made me feel like my dream of traveling wasn't crazy.

The book also talked about how most people believe you have to be rich in order to live this lifestyle.

Which is very untrue. It is actually cheaper for me to live this way than if I lived in a house.

I have less bills, less possessions that can rule over me, and the need to keep up with the Joneses is non-existent.

I need less money to live, I don't have to work as hard and I get to travel to all corners of the country as a bonus!

In determining how much I needed to save prior to full time traveling, I needed to figure out what expenses I would have each month.

I also needed to know what expenses I could pay for prior to leaving town. My truck and trailer insurance is one of those bills. I was able to pay for a full year in advance. This way I don't have to worry about that expense each month.

Here is my budget:

(Medical, dental and veterinarian expenses I did not budget for)

Description	Monthly Cost	Yearly Cost
Auto/trailer insurance		$950
Fuel	$200	
Campground Fees	$1,000	
Boondockers Welcome		$40
Harvest Hosts		$70
Good Sams Club		$30
KOA Rewards Card		$35
Entertainment	$300	
Truck maintenance		$5,000
Food	$300	
Toiletries/Laundry	$50	
Cell Phone	$150	
Total	$2,000	

You don't want to get out on the road and realize that you didn't budget enough money.

I have been keeping daily costs below my budgeted amount because of high truck repair costs I've been riddled with.

I wasn't really anticipating vehicle trouble so early in my trip. My truck was in three different auto shops within the first month on the road. And each shop was in a different state! I have already spent my budget on truck maintenance...no bueno.

I will have to start earning an income within the next couple of months in order to maintain my lifestyle. I will cover working from the road in Chapter Four.

While I was collecting money in order to save up twelve months of the budgeted amount, I made sure to put that money in a separate bank account.

When I came into some unexpected cash, and I didn't need it for bills, I would put it into my travel account.

I know it's difficult, but try not to touch that money once you put it into your travel account. It's surprising how much you can save, little by little.

One trick I wished I would have utilized was the round-up tool one of my banks offered. For every purchase you make, the bank will round up that amount and put the difference into your savings account. That would have added up without me even knowing it!

If you are working full time and don't have the extra cash to save, I would suggest getting a part time job. Working hard for a year or two so you can put money in your travel account is so worth it!

Keeping your monthly costs down is your goal!

If you have any debt you will need to ask yourself how you will be paying those bills.

Will you be able to pay them off prior to traveling full time?

If not, do you have enough saved or will you be earning enough on the road to pay those bills monthly?

Can you sell something like a house or car in order to pay off your debt?

These are all questions you need to ask yourself while putting together your plan.

I was able to sell my business, ATV, and Jaguar prior to leaving town. All that money went right into my travel account. It didn't add up to much but every little bit helps!

And remember that budgets are meant as a guideline. Monitoring and adjusting that budget once on the road is imperative. Things come up that you were not expecting, and those costs need to be tracked and accounted for.

I noticed my gas budget fluctuated considerably. Over a month's time I was either going from state to state, or I was staying in the same RV park for a full month. Both of those scenarios affect my gas budget.

It also affects my campground fee's. If I'm staying in one place for a month, the rates are much cheaper.

If I'm using Boondockers Welcome or Harvest Hosts then my stay is free. Some of the hosts with both those programs may charge for power or ask that you purchase items from them.

For those of you who are unaware of these programs, I give you all the details you need to decide if they are for you in Chapter Seven; including other resources for planning where to stay.

Sometimes, though, if you stay in one location for too long, you start to relax and you begin to eat out more and partake in all that that area has to offer.

Be careful not to exceed your budget during these month-long stays!

My only constant monthly cost is my cell phone bill. I have a cell phone and a large iPad. They both have unlimited data and a personal hotspot. When I say unlimited data, it just means they won't charge me if I use more than the cell company thinks I should. Because after I've surpassed that amount, they slow my data down.

If I'm in an area that does not offer free wifi, then I sparingly use the hotspot on my ipad. I try to save my phone data so I'm able to use my phone without having the data slowed down.

I use my iPad primarily for a television. I have Amazon Prime which allows me to download any movies that I have purchased, or some of the free movies, or tv shows that prime allows me. Once downloaded on my iPad, I'm able to watch movies or tv shows without any data use or internet. It's pretty cool!

One item I did have on my original needs list was a new laptop, but that was not in the budget prior to me leaving, nor is it in the budget now.

But I do have one of my son's old laptops, that is missing a button on the keyboard. Again, doesn't bother me having a hand me down. It does the job, and has allowed me to save money.

I'm writing this book on it!

Now let's talk about credit cards.

I have a couple of credit cards. Two with very low credit limits and two with higher limits.

What I have found to be useful is to use the two lower limit cards for gas, this way if the number is stolen the thieves won't get too far on $300, and it protects the money in my travel account.

I use the higher credit limit cards to reserve my campgrounds and for groceries. Again, to protect my travel account, and it is also a great budgeting tool.

I just have to look at the credit card statements for my monthly expenses for each line item.

But if you do use this type of budgeting please be sure to pay off your credit card balances each month!

I sometimes pay off the balance weekly. This will be good for your credit score and it will allow you to have credit available in case something happens on the road; an unexpected emergency!

When my truck broke down on the road, three times to be exact, I had not paid off my credit card weekly and had to use my travel account card. Which meant I also had to transfer money from savings to checking. And my bank declined my charge until I was able to contact them to verify the purchase.

Both my banks and credit card companies know I'm traveling, but sometimes they will decline your purchase until you can verify it. Especially if you have driven through two states in the same week.

I also made sure to spread out my money into two separate banks prior to traveling. This way if one of your accounts is hacked you still have money in the other account. Same with credit cards.

You know the saying...don't put all your eggs in one basket.

That is so true when traveling! You don't want to be stranded on the side of the road with no gas and no place to stay because someone hacked your only bank account.

And because I'm a paranoid realist, I also have cash and coins hidden in my truck and trailer. I have coins, large bills and a lot of dollar bills.

If the banking system collapses or if I get stuck in a town with cash-only stores, I'm prepared!

And if it's the end of the world and someone is selling water bottles for a dollar, I sure won't expect that guy to have change for a hundred.

Chapter Four

Working from the road

If you do not have enough saved or have access to unlimited funds before you hit the road, you may want to think about working while traveling.

- Will your current employer allow you to work from home, aka your home on wheels?
- Can you secure an online job prior to leaving on your travels?
- Will you look for work on the road in the towns you visit?
- Is there another way to earn money while traveling? Make sure it's legal and ethical!

For me, at some point within the first six month, I will need to earn money while on the road. One way I plan to do that is writing!

One of my goals is to finish writing the multiple books and screenplays that I have already started. Some of them I've been working on for over twenty years!

I'm also going to start submitting articles to magazines; online and print.

At some RV parks or camp grounds they hire their tenants to help take care of the premises.

And if you are following the sun and staying in resort towns there are a lot of seasonal or temporary jobs available to you.

It's on my bucket list to be a bartender. I'm sure if I stay in a town for a month or so I could get a temporary job helping at a bar during the day. I could check something off my bucket list and earn some extra cash too!

Another idea I have to earn money is to write and illustrate children's books which I would then sell at farmers markets, or book fairs.

If you have a talent for painting, or making jewelry, selling those wares would be a great way to supplement your travel expenses as well!

A few of the resources I have found that can help you start working online from the road are:

- Upwork
- Fiverr
- Flexjobs
- Freeup
- Guru
- PeoplePerHour
- Hubstaff Talent
- Freelancer

Of course, there are new online sites sprouting up every day so I would search the internet weekly to see what's new.

Working at home or remotely is on the rise!

You can also earn money on YouTube if you can get a certain number of subscribers and have people watch a certain number of minutes of your uploaded videos.

I have two YouTube channels that I have started working on. In retrospect I should have built up my viewer base prior to me hitting the road. But alas...I did not.

Travelintoxication and Life of Parley are my two YouTube channels. I post on them weekly. I'm an amateur at it, but I'm getting better...I hope.

(selfless plug: go to my YouTube channels and hit subscribe and watch all the videos...all of them)

Back in early 2016 I created a blog titled Travelintoxication. There I started writing about my five-year plan, among other things.

This is a free blog site, and readers can sign up for my email list to be notified when I publish a new post. *(subliminal message: go to travelintoxication.com and sign up...it's free)*

Some bloggers charge to read their blogs. If you feel you have a blog that shares information that readers cannot get anywhere else, you may be able to charge a fee for them to access it. It could be a single use fee, monthly fee or yearly fee. It's all dependent upon the content you are selling.

In my travels I have also met those who choose to work seasonally. They travel to various farms and work for a season in order to fund their traveling for the rest of the year.

On one of my many trips back from Vegas, my friends and I met a couple who traveled to different parts of the world where marijuana was legal to work at various farms.

He was a scientist who could engineer new types of marijuana plants. He got paid well, and he and his girlfriend were able to fly all over the world, essentially free travel. They were heading to Washington State to work on a farm because they had always wanted to see the state.

During this pandemic there is a need at many hospitals and clinics for nurses and nurse's assistants. Some of the fellow travelers in multiple RV parks I have stayed in had temporary medical staff as customers.

The few who I talked with sold their homes, bought an RV and started the full-time traveling life. All while helping out communities within the United States that needed help with Covid.

I'm sure I have not even scratched the surface on ways to make money while traveling, but I hope that this will give you some ideas to assist you in making the decision on what you will do for money on the road, if you need it.

Chapter Five

Assets – House, Land, Vehicle, Boat

This chapter is about large assets. Not about grandma's doily, or your gold wedding silverware, but about homes, land, boats and cars.

The next thing to decide on before hitting the road is what you will do with your large assets.

Do you own your home?

Are you going to rent it out or sell it?

If you will be selling it you may not sell it right away, or you may sell it too quickly. Have a plan for both of these scenarios.

If you plan to rent your home will you have someone manage the renters for you? A property manager? A reliable friend?

What happens if the house needs repairs? How will you pay for those repairs?

What if your tenant stops paying rent, or moves out?

Have these details written into your plan prior to you leaving town.

If you do not own your own home, where are you living now?

Do you rent your house or apartment? When is your lease up?

Do you have roommates that rely on your rent??

When I finally decided on my set-in-stone leave date I made sure to tell my roommates six months in advance that I was moving out. We were renting a large house, and I made sure my leave date was after our lease was up.

If you have property that needs to be managed or maintained, how will you do that from the road?

How many vehicles do you own? Will you be selling those vehicles?

Will you be storing them? Where will you store them? Is there a cost to that?

Who will maintain those vehicles?

Same with a boat.

Will you sell your boat? Store it??

Is it a large boat that you have to pay a moorage fee?

Who will maintain your boat?

After I had purchased my truck, I was a two-vehicle family. I had an older Jaguar and a truck. I knew that I was going to sell my car, even though I loved that car, and it was a great running vehicle. But I didn't want to store it, and I needed the money I would get from selling it for my travel fund.

It ended up that one of my best friends purchased the car from me...win win!

As with the sale of any of these items, selling them will be an artform. You will need to figure out how long you think it will take you to sell each item. You won't want to sell your house too soon, because then where will you live? In your trailer or motorhome perhaps??

All of these decisions will need to be included in your plan, and if you are receiving large sums of money from these sales, I suggest you use it to pay off all your debt and save the rest for traveling. Just my two cents.

Chapter Six

The rest of your belongings

If you are like most Americans you have a lot of stuff. We Americans know how to consume!

What will you be doing with all that stuff you have in your house, in your car, and in your storage unit?

You probably can't take it all with you.

You can always put it in storage, but that will add another monthly bill to your budget.

Remember, you will need to keep those monthly costs low.

I had been downsizing every couple of months for several years in anticipation of this adventure I was going on. I had numerous garage sales over the years and sold items on online markets. And I donated a lot of my stuff to charity organizations...a lot of it!

I got my inspiration and encouragement to purge from a book about minimalism, and how to downsize your belongings.

The book was an easy read, and every time I read a chapter in that book it put a fire under me to get rid of things. I would fill up at least one garbage bag a month with items that I would donate to charity.

From clothes to knickknacks to shoes and purses...nothing was sacred.

I will admit, however, that the sentimental items were the hardest to part with. But in that minimalism book they talked about how we are attached to the memories of an item, not the actual item.

With that knowledge in mind, I setup a studio in my garage and I took really nice pictures of all of the items I was getting rid of. I thought that I could order a book of those pictures so that I could see them and remember the memories just by opening the book. I still have not made that picture book because I have not missed those items at all. Out of sight out of mind.

I did have some items that I was unwilling to part with; three bins of items to be exact...and my childhood wrought iron bed frame.

I thankfully talked my parents into allowing me to store the three bins and my bed frame at their house. If I had not had that option, then those three bins and the bed frame would have been traveling with me in the bed of my truck, bed frame and all!

I knew I wasn't going to rent a storage space for my items. I would not have been able to afford it. But if you have the funds and you have items you just can't let go of then storage units are the way to go.

You can also hit up family or friends to see if they can help you out by storing your items, that is the cheapest option.

Pictures were also an issue for me. I had so many picture albums! My solution was to take all of those photos out of the photo albums, sell those empty albums and then digitize all of my pictures. To say that it was a time-consuming project is an understatement!

I looked into scanners but decided that I would take a picture of the picture with my cell phone. And I have backed up all of those pictures with Google Photos and on an external hard drive!

First, I sorted all of my pictures into different categories. For example, childhood pictures, pictures of my mom's side of the family, pictures of my dad's side of the family, pictures of my son, pictures of various groups of friends, and the list goes on and on.

I took pictures of each category with my cell phone and then placed those photos into large marked manilla envelopes.

Before the pandemic we were able to celebrate Christmas as a family. I brought my mom's side of the family's envelope of pictures and spread them out on my aunts table before dinner. They were a hit! My family had so much fun looking at old and new photos. I told them to take any picture they wanted because I did not want them back.

I did this for all of the photo groupings. It was so fun to see family and friends smiling and reliving memories together, just from seeing those photos. It was satisfying...and I got rid of all my pictures!

The photo project took me about six months.

Before my leave date I still had a bedroom, living room, half a kitchen and half a garage full of stuff that I needed to get rid of. It almost looked like I hadn't downsized at all, but I had, I swear it!

So, the weekend before I left town, I had a very large garage sale. Because of the pandemic, masks were worn, and the amount of people who shopped was high! I sold almost everything except for what I was taking on my trip...the rest went out in the yard with a free sign on it, to charity or to the dump.

I made almost $400 from the sale of my belongings. My friends and family also brought items to sell which made it a huge sale.

This gave me coins and cash that I needed to hide around my truck and trailer...and some more quarters for laundry.

I had also sold my ATV to one of my good friends. More cash for my travels.

Plus, after you liquidate all of your belongings, it's harder to back out of your leave date.

For me, I knew that after the garage sale, I couldn't turn back on my dream of traveling...it was about to get real.

Chapter Seven

Planning your route...or wander aimlessly

Most RV'ers have a general idea of where they would like to go and how long they would like to stay in each place. Others want to just drive where the wind takes them.

I already knew the first few destinations that I was going to travel to, but now I go where the wind and sun take me.

Some of the apps that I use to plan my routes are:

- RoadTrippers
- Allstays
- KOA
- Apple Maps
- Campendium

I have found that you cannot rely on just one app to plan your trip. You need multiple sources to help you decide the path you will be driving and where you will be staying for the night.

There is a cost associated with a few of these apps, but I have found that they are well worth the money.

Before I decide on a location, I look at how many miles I will have to drive to get there. I do not want most of this adventure to be spent driving. So, I limit my miles to under 250 miles a day.

And if I've felt that I have been driving too much, I have even reduced that number to 74 miles in one day. Especially if I have multiple stops I want to make along the way.

I also have a rule that I do not drive at night. It's just not worth it to me. Even though I did break that rule twice, I will do everything in my power to not break it again.

Because, again, I am a paranoid realist, there are more things that could go wrong at night on the side of the road in the middle of nowhere than at high noon on the side of the road in the middle of nowhere.

If you are going to be staying at campgrounds, RV parks, or using the countless apps for travelers, you will need to make reservations typically a day or two in advance. Sometimes you are lucky and can roll in on the day of, but have a plan B in case there is no vacancy.

As a solo female traveler, safety is always my number one concern when finding a place to stay for the night.

Earlier in the book I talked about Boondockers Welcome and Harvest Hosts. Another program I will talk about here is called Hip Camp.

Boondockers Welcome (boondockerswelcome.com) is a program that allows regular people to open up their driveway, property, or on the street in front of their house to travelers needing a safe and free place to sleep for the night.

Some of the Boondockers Welcome hosts will allow you to stay up to five nights, and most allow you to hook up to their power. I have utilized this a couple of times, and it was a very positive experience.

Harvest Hosts (harvesthosts.com) is another program that I use. It allows you to stay the night at wineries, breweries, distilleries, family farms or ranches.

The stay is free, and some hosts will allow you to stay up to three nights, and some provide power. They just ask if you could support their business while staying there.

I have stayed at a family farm with a pig who sits on command for a cookie! It was an amazing experience.

I also purchased fresh eggs, and they served me a fresh breakfast for a cost! It was very reasonably priced! I was happy, the small farm was happy and most importantly the pig was happy!

It has not worked out for me to stay at a winery yet, but I'm sure it won't take me long to find one on my travel path within the next couple of months!

Hipcamp (hipcamp.com) is another program that has seemed to have sprang up from thin air. The best way I can describe it is it's similar to AirBnB, but for RV'ers. It has some amazing locations with some very affordable pricing. And there is typically no limit for the amount of time you are able to stay at each location. At one of the places I booked through Boondockers Welcome I met a fellow traveler who was parked next to me in the hosts driveway. He told me that he booked his stay through Hipcamp. He was able to rent each night for $13 and could stay as long as he wanted to. While my stay was free, I was only allowed to stay for one night.

All three of these programs have hosts throughout the United States and into Canada. And they are always adding new hosts.

There are other free places to stay around the United States. Bureau of Land Management land is one of them. It is federal land that your taxes pay to keep up, so in a sense, it's your land. You are able to stay on most federal land for up to two weeks, free of charge.

The trade-off is that there are no hookups, no pools, and typically no bathrooms or showers.

You must be able to boondock in order to take advantage of the free stay.

State Parks are also an inexpensive place to stay. Most of them have electrical and water hookups, and a dump station on site. Some have bathrooms, showers and laundry facilities.

Each state maintains their own parks, which means each park will have different rules and different amenities.

Private campgrounds or RV parks are everywhere!

Most of the private parks that I've stayed in have been amazing, but there was one campground that I actually left after staying only one night there. I had already paid for two nights. It looked like people lived there full time with no rules. There was garbage and dog poop all over my campsite. The trailer next to me had an actual couch in their campsite.

In order for me to avoid booking those types of campgrounds in the future I make sure to do two things; I read the independent reviews of the campground and I go to my mapping software and look at the satellite view of the park. You can tell a lot from that type of view.

I also look at the satellite view on my Roadtrippers app. And I'll tell you why.

Before booking the wonderful RV park I am currently staying in for two months in Texas, I looked at the satellite view of the park.

To my surprise the photo showed the park just after it was hit by a hurricane! All I could see was trailers and motorhomes laying on their sides with palm tree branches all over the park.

So, I went to one of my other apps to get a more recent view of the park. That one showed nice green grass, and a very clean RV park.

To book most of the campgrounds or RV parks you will have to call them directly. Which has been nice because then I can ask them questions about their sites and amenities.

In turn, it makes checking in so much more personable since you have already talked with the front office about your needs, and they have already let you know the park rules.

I also suggest not booking your sites too far into the future. You may want to stay longer in certain campgrounds, and if you are booked too far in advance in numerous campgrounds it would be a nightmare trying to change or cancel all of those reservations.

Because of the pandemic the United States has seen a huge shift where people are leaving their homes to live full time in their RV's. This leaves campgrounds and RV parks with fewer vacancies, more rules and most have even raised their rates.

I have experienced no vacancies at certain RV parks, parks that only allow one pet, or parks who do not allow older trailers in. Don't be surprised if these things happen to you, too, just know that there are many other amazing places to stay.

Stay positive and just go with the flow of it all. Remember, you are living your dream!

48

Chapter Eight

Protection of life and property

This is where I can help to mitigate all of those fears you and your loved ones may have about your dream of traveling.

Insurance can be your friend.

Before embarking on this adventure, call your insurance agent and let them know what you are planning to do.

There is such a thing as full time RV insurance...yes, it's a thing.

This insurance policy will cover your truck AND your trailer. Because now your trailer is your home. My policy pays up to $4,000 for any lost, damaged or stolen property out of my truck and trailer. It will also pay for a tow truck if I break down. Unlike AAA, it will pay to have both my truck and trailer towed if I break down.

Make sure you are truthful to your insurance agent and get a policy that covers your needs.

My insurance company told me that if I lie about living in my RV that they will not cover any costs and my policy would be null and void.

A little harsh, I think, but all the more reason not to lie about what you are planning on doing. Plus, the cost of the full time RV policy is fairly priced.

Personal safety and situational awareness are something to take very seriously. If you ever find yourself in a campground or an area where you feel uncomfortable or something or someone makes you feel like something just isn't right...leave.

I have left a campground that I did not feel comfortable in. It wasn't worth it to me to stay and be on edge the whole night.

I try to always be situationally aware at all times. I watch what others are doing; I make sure to pay attention instead of burying myself into my phone or a book when I'm out in public.

If a stranger approaches me, I gauge the situation by using my gut. I'm not afraid to tell someone to leave or back off.

I will put the palm of my hand up towards their face and boldly ask them to walk away or I will call the police.

I look people in the eye and try to make myself appear bigger and bolder. And taller than my five feet.

I take the power away from the stranger and I use it to ensure my safety if I feel threatened even in the least.

Be bold, be strong and be aware.

Even though most of the United States is safe, there is always that one place, or that one incident that can make you question humanity and your safety.

Before you encounter a situation where you feel vulnerable, think about what you will use to ensure your personal safety.

Guns are typically what travelers gravitate towards, but they can be tricky. Each state has different laws surrounding guns. Make sure to know the gun laws in each state you will be traveling through.

Just know that if you take your gun out and point it at a threat, that means that you are willing to take another person's life. Are you ready to make that decision?

Mace, pepper spray or bear spray is another option. Ensure you know how to utilize these items before you are forced to use them. If used improperly you could cause more damage to yourself than to the threat you are trying to disable.

Baseball bats, or other types of hand to hand combat weapons can be useful too.

Even having multiple or all of these types of weapons at your disposal should make you feel more confident in defending yourself.

Dogs are a huge deterrent and a great warning, tool! Even smaller dogs can be affective.

My little dog barks if someone gets too close to the truck or trailer, or if the cats try to eat his food. Either way it allows me to be situationally aware of my surroundings.

My dog also likes to bark and growl in his sleep, so at night I've often woken due to one of his dreams making him bark.

But at least I know I wake up when he barks!

And I know where my weapons of choice are even when I'm half asleep. Even if it's in the middle of the night and it scares the crap out of me.

Tracking systems are another good tool to utilize.

My family and friends have an app on our phones called Life360. This app tracks your phone whereabouts down to the part of a building you're in. It's scary accurate.

But if I go missing, my parents, son, cousins, and a handful of friends can relay my phones location to the police on my behalf. Or at least the last known location of my phone.

I also have a SPOT that tracks me by using satellites, not cell service. It has a panic button on the device in case I need help immediately.

I keep both the SPOT and my cell phone near my bed each night. Both on their chargers.

When I'm driving, I also have both near me in the truck, and on their chargers.

Safety to me also includes fire safety.

Install a small fire extinguisher near your kitchen area and install a smoke and carbon monoxide detector, too.

Most trailers and motorhomes will go up in flames within seconds. Having a warning system may give you the time you need to get out of the fire safely.

Nothing is guaranteed of course, but you probably have those items in your home, why wouldn't you install them in your home on wheels.

Another hazard on the road is weather.

It's something we cannot control, but we can certainly avoid it.

Hurricanes, flooding, earthquakes, tornado's, snow storms and extremely hot temperatures.

All of these things can turn a good time into a bad time!

One app that I utilize to monitor weather is the FEMA app. I can add locations into the app, and if there is a weather advisory in that area, it will send me an alert. It's a great tool!

The Weather app on my phone is also very helpful. It will alert me to windy days approaching, or rain, or heat.

It helps me decide if I need to put down my awning, watch for water leaks inside the trailer or if I need to get my a/c unit hooked up!

Asking the locals about the weather in their area is very beneficial as well.

Be safe out there people!!

Chapter Nine

Mail

One big issue that full time RV travelers have is figuring out how to get their mail while on the road.

There are multiple vendors out there that will help you with that. Numerous mail services will receive, scan and email your mail to you.

If you need that mail to physically appear in your hands, those same services can mail your package to wherever you are in the United States.

All of that for a fee of course.

So, what did I do? I of course called mom and dad.

They allowed me to setup my permanent address at their house. Their address is on all of my legal paperwork, cell phone account, credit card accounts, bank accounts...everything.

If I am staying in a town for a month I can go to the local postal office and rent a mailbox for one month, then have my parents send me a package with my mail in it. Or they open my mail for me, and just send me a picture of what I received. It's worked out so far.

If I order something from Amazon, they have places of business all over the country where you can get packages delivered to and you are able to go pick up your package by showing ID, and the secret number Amazon send you to show proof that it's your package. It works really well!

Some campground offices will also allow you to receive mail or packages at the main office. But you need to verify this with the RV park or campground you are at.

Important papers

How much paperwork do you have in those file cabinets at your home?

Do you have your tax records from 1970 until now in shoe boxes like my dad??

If so, what will you do with all that paperwork?

Just like my belongings, I also began going through all of the file boxes I had just sitting in the garage. Three to be exact.

I was able to get down to one hard cased snoopy suitcase which is currently stored in my trailer by my shoes.

I scanned into my computer all of the paperwork that I did not need an original copy or paper copy of.

I also had copies of my titles for my truck and trailer, which I made sure to give my parents a copy of each of those, and also of my driver's license and passport. Just in case they needed those things while I was on the road...you just never know.

Decide what you believe you will need while on your adventure. Scanning in most documents is sufficient, but items like your certified birth certificate isn't one that you can just scan in.

There are so many things you can do online now that most of your paperwork is not needed. For example, bank statements or credit card bills.

Both of those can be found online.

Will or power of attorney

Do you have a will? And in that will do you list a power of attorney?

If not, what happens to all your stuff if you die, or are incapacitated while on the road?

Remember earlier in the book I talked about death coming to get you when it's your time?

Well, what if your time comes while you are on the road??

Having a will and a power of attorney will make things easier for those that you leave behind.

In one of the RV parks I stayed in the gentleman whose trailer was a couple sites down from mine died. It took a few weeks for his trailer to be towed away, and I believe it was his sister who showed up trying to get her brothers estate in order.

Having a plan in place with your travel partners would also be beneficial.

I sometimes think about what would happen if I died in my trailer, who would take my pets, how would anyone even know that I died.

All of these questions can be discussed with your loved ones, and the camp hosts would worry about me at most of the campgrounds if they didn't see me come out of my trailer every day.

Something to think about...

Chapter Ten

Rodents and bugs

Hopefully this chapter doesn't scare you. But if you aren't careful, you could get over run with little critters and bugs in your new living space.

I have watched numerous videos on YouTube of full time RV'ers taking nighttime videos of little mice or large rats running amuck inside their trailers or motorhomes. This can be a huge problem. The little critters want to find warmth, and food. Or air conditioning and water, or all of those things.

Make sure you have holes in your living space sealed up as best you can. Set mouse or rat traps or bait out to detour them from staying in your living space.

Snakes also would love to come into your living space if they want to warm up or cool off. Make sure to prepare by researching what types of snakes are in your area, and if they are poisonous or not. I have even heard rumors of snakes coming up through septic hoses and into your toilet...urban legend I think, but nonetheless a scary thought.

Ants have been a constant problem at numerous campgrounds I have stayed in. Even the really nice ones!

Waking up by being bitten and walked over by ants in your bed does not make for a nice morning. I had to set out ant traps and use ant spray to apply to all of the contact points between my trailer and the ground. I had to reapply that spray every couple of days, too.

If you are traveling with pets and/or kids, remember to make sure they do not ingest that ant spray.

Mosquitos and flies have also been a problem. I have a screen door and I inspect my window screens regularly to make sure bugs cannot get in that way. I also have bug spray that I can spray on myself if they bother me while outside.

Some bugs are unidentifiable. One day I opened up the storage under my table seats and a large bug with wings jumped down from the top of the stuff...I just ignored it. Grabbed what I needed and closed it back up. I guess I was just hoping he would take the hint and leave. Probably wishful thinking.

To take care of all of the above, or keep them out of my trailer, I have faith in my two secret weapons...my cats.

My two cats catch and eat any bugs we have in the trailer, and I'm pretty sure that if a mouse or rat decided to sniff around in the trailer, he would be either chased out or killed. Snakes on the other hand I watch for, that and scorpions. I don't want my pets to be injured by those demons.

Wild animals

There may be places that you will be staying that have wild animals nearby or running through your campsite. Whether it be bears, wolves, coyotes, cougars or gators, educating yourself on those hazards before you go to those areas will be beneficial. Especially if you have pets or small children with you.

One campground had coyotes running through it once the sun goes down until it comes up again.

I make sure to walk my dog when it is light out, or if I do need to give him a potty break when it's dark, I keep him on a short leash and I'm very aware of my surroundings.

Some boondocking locations allow you to let your animals run off leash, but make sure that they will come back when called, and never let them roam alone at night. I always keep my dog and cats on leashes with long leads. This way I am able to pull them back up into my arms if I need too. But you know your pets better than anyone, it is up to you to decide if it's worth the risk to let them run free.

Chapter Eleven

Significant other

I have seen numerous ads online for t-shirts with the words, "I'm sorry for what I said when I was backing up the trailer."
This is a popular item because it's true.
If you are already fighting with your significant other in a house, think about how your relationship will be after you move into a trailer or motorhome.
I have witnessed numerous couples arguing loudly in many RV parks and campgrounds.
But I have also witnessed numerous couples fighting while I lived in suburbia too.
But just know that your current problems will be magnified living in smaller quarters. And traveling full time can be stressful, which can affect your relationship.
Prior to driving off into the sunset with your significant other in a trailer, motorhome or whatever you choose to travel in, make sure to have an open and honest discussion.
Some topics to discuss are who is going to do what. Have a division of jobs. Maybe you like to do laundry and your significant other likes to do the dishes.
You can find out who likes what during your practice camp outs prior to leaving town on your adventure.

Where will you go and what will you see is another topic to discuss at length. Having a clear vision of what both of your goals are, and making sure those goals jive, is imperative.

You don't want to get on the road and realize that your goals and expectations are completely different.

You don't want to be seen wearing a t-shirt that says, "I'm not sorry you're an idiot" while on the road, do you?

Family or Friends

Most of the above can also apply if you will be traveling with your sister, or mother, or a good friend.

Agreeing on a plan prior to your leave date will hopefully alleviate some of the problems that could arise.

Children

I do not have young children, but when my son was young we went on a very long road trip.

I can only imagine if we lived on the road and what I would have to do to prepare myself and my child

There are quite a few families who are traveling full time with their children. A few of the families I have watched YouTube videos of had four to six children.

If you decide to travel full time with your kids there are a few things to figure out prior to leaving town.

School. Nowadays most schools are conducted online, but once the pandemic is over, will you homeschool your children?

Have you acquired a large enough vehicle and/or living space on wheels to accommodate your family?

How will you handle their belongings? Will your children be responsible for downsizing those belongings?

If you have a baby or toddler what safety precautions have you taken to ensure they will be safe within your living space on the road.

Have you prepared your children mentally for full time traveling? It may seem like a vacation at the beginning of your adventure, but after a few months, it will sink in that this is now your lifestyle.

64

Chapter Twelve

Pets

Traveling with a small dog and two big cats in a small vintage trailer has been an adventure in itself.

My dog Parley loves to travel, he has since I adopted him from a shelter almost two years ago. He absolutely loves to ride in the truck and gets really mad if I don't take him with me.

As for my cats, Sydney and Murray, I actually was not planning on adopting more cats after mine passed away. But here we are...two cats strong!

When I adopted my cats, they were little kittens. I took them in the truck and car for rides at least every other week in order to get them used to it. I also bought harnesses and leashes for both cats. They are both leash trained.

With any pet that you decide to take with you on your adventure you should talk with your vet about your plans in order to ensure they remain healthy on the trip.

In Washington state we do not have heartworms, but in many other states they do. So, Parley's vet started him on a monthly dose of heartworm meds prior to my leave date. And they gave me enough pills for a full year.

The dog and both cats had all of their shots prior to my leave date, and I have brought their rabies certificates and tags.

So far only one campground asked for their paperwork, which I was glad to show them, as I keep their tags in my purse at all times and I have an app on my phone that holds all of their medical history and certificates.

While traveling, I am always aware of where the nearest veterinary clinics are, just in case.

Pet supplies are a must!

I have a bag that I keep in the truck that has a baggie full of cat food, a baggie full of dog food, food bowls for each pet, a large water bowl, leashes, dog poop bags and most important bottled water.

In the back of my truck I have a large container with a lid that contains dog food, extra plastic tubs of kitty litter and a mid-size cooler bag full of cat food.

I have about three of those awesome cooler bags. Once they start leaking when full of ice, I make sure to find other uses for them...like holding cat food.

In my trailer I have a cloth bag my mom made me which is full of more dog poop bags, dog shampoo and heartworm medication. It is hanging just inside the door along with numerous leashes and tie-out cables.

Under the trailer table I have a little bin of toys; dog and cat. Under the sink I have little treat containers full of treats.

Having supplies spread out into both my truck and my trailer is vital. With pets it's good to be overly prepared!

Most of these supplies I purchased prior to leaving. It was easy to collect these items from friends, discount stores and garage sales.

The only items I have had to replenish on the road is dog food, cat food and kitty litter.

Prior to my leave date I also purchased a large wire ferret cage for the cats. I set it up in my backyard and let them get used to it for a couple months prior to leaving.

Plus, it took me that long to figure out an easy way to fold it down and put it up. I only pinched and almost broke my fingers a few times...no biggie.

I keep a litter box in the cage along with water and little blankets that cover the shelves for them to sit on I've also tied a cat toy from the top of the cage so they have something to bat at.

Most campgrounds will allow me to put the cat cage up, but some have strict rules against it. Plus, I only set the large cage up if I'm going to be in the same spot for more than three days.

In those instances, I put the halters on the cats and tie them out in front of the trailer. I have to be out there with them as I don't trust them to not try to back out of their halters.

I have also purchased a nylon dog crate with screens on two sides. This is a life saver! It folds flat, is light weight and the cats love it.

For Parley I have a short tie-out cable and a long one. The short one I use to tie him up to the trailer stairs. The long one I use when we are in the woods, at the beach or in a place that has plenty of room for him to roam.

While driving from spot to spot I have all three pets inside the cab of the truck. I have a booster seat for Parley that I am able to tie him into. I have a backpack that both cats go into any time I am transferring them from the trailer to the truck.

While visiting locations that allow pets, like the Grand Canyon, I had Parley on his leash and I had Sydney and Murray in their backpack on my back.

I've also taken them all into pet stores and hardware stores, too. They love it, and people are always a little startled when Murray starts meowing from the back pack.

Which takes me to my next topic...pets and heat.

Many times while traveling, I have had to get supplies at stores that do not allow pets. And I have some rules about this.

If it is over 80 degrees outside I will not leave the pets in the truck, or in the trailer while I'm in a store. I just have to wait, or if I can run in and out of the store within 10 minutes then I leave the a/c on in the truck and lock both doors. (I have two sets of keys for everything)

Early in the beginning of my travels I had two days of driving with no a/c because it had broken in my truck. It was 120 degrees out and I was not able to stop and cool down for any length of time. We powered through it, and my pets were kept cool by pouring water on them. Sounds horrible, and it was.

I felt terrible about it too. That type of thing won't happen again. Lesson learned.

I also do not put the pets in the trailer while we are driving down the road unless it's absolutely necessary. It can be very dangerous for them. Things in my trailer haven fallen, or spilled out of cupboards, and it can be extremely hot inside.

One day both cats leapt out of the trailer and took off running! I shook the treat container and Murray came back for some treats, but Sydney went missing for a few days.

After putting flyers up all around the campground, canvassing all of the surrounding areas and talking with most of the other campers we were able to get her back.

A couple found her a mile away on the side of the road and through Facebook found someone who had seen the missing cat flyers at the campground. She used one of her nine lives that trip.

After retrieving Sydney, we all took a trip to the nearest pet store. Both cats now have a collar with a tag that has their name and my phone number on it. Just in case this happens again.

Parley also has a harness with tags on at all times except when we go to sleep, he is also microchipped.

So, having collars or harnesses with tags may help you get your pet back if they run off like Sydney did.

Something to keep in mind while traveling with dogs is that they will need to be walked at least three times a day. Some campgrounds have specific areas where you can take your pet to go the bathroom, other campgrounds have fully fenced dog parks. Parley loves the dog parks, and he loves going on his daily walks...all of them.

I have also taken the cats to a dog park. They also loved it! But if you do take your cats to one, first make sure there are no other dogs there, and in some instances you will need to check with camp host to make sure it is ok.

Nice campgrounds are very strict about where your dog can do his business so make sure you know the rules prior to booking your site.

If you are boondocking out in the woods, desert, or swamp on federal or state land make sure you watch your pets at all times whether they are on leash or off.

I would hate to hear about your pet being killed by the wild animals in the area. Or if you allow your dog off leash and they don't come back, what is your plan? Can you shake a treat container to get them back?

As I said in a previous chapter, be situationally aware at all times, especially if you are taking your pet's life in your own hands.

Bathing your pet is something to think about as well. If you have a large bathroom with a tub, or even a nice sized shower, this would solve that problem. But if you have a small or no bathroom at all, you will need to figure out where you will give your pet a bath.

I have a small bathroom that has a toilet and a handheld shower head above it...it's about the size of a closet.

I use my collapsible laundry basket to bathe Parley. I place it on top of my toilet, place him in the basket and utilize the shower head to give him a bath. I have a drain in the bathroom floor for all the water to go after I dump out that laundry basket. Be prepared for water to be everywhere after such a bath.

Most campgrounds do not allow pets inside of their bath houses. And yes, this includes your pet. You do not want to get caught and get kicked out of your site.

Travelers in vans have told me that they typically go to a lake to bathe their dogs, or they will find a dog groomer. If you do use a groomer, make sure that expense is in your budget.

Finally, the biggest question I have gotten is...where is the kitty litter box?

It took me months and months to figure this out.

When I first started traveling, I had a small grey dish tub as a litter box, and I placed it under my bed with a small mat to collect any litter off their paws. My cats got too big, so I had to purchase a larger corner litter box. This one works like a champ! I also bought a larger mat to collect the litter off their paws. I have a scooper that came in a standup holder that closes.

I have talked with travelers with larger trailers that have large storage bays on the side of their trailers. They installed kitty doors so their cats can go from the trailer into the storage container. There they have their litter boxes and extra litter.

In order to ensure that you are not smelling the litter box you will need to scoop it at least every other day, if not every day.

I also suggest buying a small handheld vacuum because no matter how big or expensive those mats are, you will still get some litter on your floor everywhere the cat walks.

The vacuum is perfect for pet hair too!

72

Chapter Thirteen

Emotionally and psychologically prepared

I don't think anything could have completely prepared me for traveling full time. When researching this lifestyle over the years I did not see one video or article talking about how difficult this can be.

I almost gave up after my first two weeks. Seriously, I did.

I talked a little about this incident earlier in the book, but here is the psychology of it all.

I had truck trouble, I was alone with my pets and they were depending on me to take care of them. The worst part was driving through 120 F degree weather, with my a/c broken in my truck, the two cats and my dog tied into the truck because both windows had to be down. I would pour water over their heads every 15 minutes or so to stop them from panting...I thought I was going to die, I thought we were all going to die.

Now in retrospect, that full day of driving was a huge lesson on what not to do. I should have broken up my drive, stopped somewhere where I could plug my trailer in to shore power and run my a/c in my trailer. Or rented a motel room that allowed pets, and then drove only in the mornings, not through the worst time of day. Lessons learned. And it showed me how tough I truly was, how resilient the animals were and how I needed to adjust how I was traveling.

For some reason I felt I was on a mission to see so many places, visit so many people, but in reality, I needed to slow down and enjoy the trip. My cats and dog would have liked that better than racing through the desert with no a/c in the truck.

If you are choosing this lifestyle, even if it's for only a year, just to escape your life, then you will be very disappointed when you hit the road.

I have all the same problems as when I left, I have to continue to work on myself, dealing with my PTSD, and in some instances have to work on my relationships that I left at home.

My family and friends support me, but it's been hard on them seeing me leave. I did feel some guilt when telling them my leave date, and then again when I actually left town.

I believe my life now is more difficult then when I was at home. I'm living in beautiful places for short spans of time, but it takes a lot of work physically as well as mentally.

I'm always aware of my surroundings, I plan and am methodical in everything I do, otherwise I could really get hurt or it could cost myself a lot of money if my actions damage my truck, trailer, pets...or me.

So please do not have any misconceptions of how traveling full time will fix your life. Because it won't. Only you can do that.

I do not want to jade or deter you from living this type of life. But I do want you to go into this with your eyes wide open

Now I will add that I do not regret living this lifestyle for anything in the world. It has taught me so much about myself, it has empowered me more than anything else I have ever done in my life. At this point I feel I can accomplish anything I put my mind too...anything.

Solo travel is very tough on you mentally. You may not talk to anyone in person for days or even weeks depending on where you are traveling.

If you have trouble asking for help from others, you may need to change that about yourself.

If you are traveling with pets, they are looking to you to keep them safe, fed and happy.

If you are traveling with children, they are also looking to you to keep them safe, fed and happy.

If you are traveling with your significant other you may need to have difficult talks, you may fight more than you did before you started to travel or your significant other may decide this life isn't for them.

Each scenario could take its toll on you psychologically...prepare yourself for that.

Over the first two months of being on the road there were over six people in my life that died back home. And I'm sure it will continue to happen. This is tough mentally because I am not there to be with friends or family during these times.

If it were an immediate family who passes away or are terminally ill, then that is something I will need to come to terms with as to what I would do...stay on the road or go back home.

I don't think that there is a right or wrong answer to some of these issues. And each scenario will be different.

But if you are able to at least begin thinking about what you would do, or how you would react, you will be ahead of the game.

Full time traveling could open up some things within yourself that you didn't even know were there. It can also force you to see and deal with things that you have been avoiding by keeping busy.

Remember, if you are struggling with life at home, or on the road, please do not hesitate to reach out to family, friends or a mental health professional.

There is no shame in getting help.

Sample Plan

Plan Name: _____

Leave Date: _____

Duration: _____

Goals:

_____
_____
_____
_____
_____
_____
_____
_____
_____
_____
_____
_____
_____
_____
_____
_____
_____
_____
_____
_____
_____
_____
_____
_____
_____
_____
_____

Needs List:

Need	Cost	Notes	Date Acquired

Budget:

Description	Monthly Cost	Yearly Cost
Total		

Income Sources:

Working from the road:

Large Assets

Housing - Own

Property manager? Yes or No

Rental fee:

Housing - Rent

Expiration date of lease:

Roommates? Yes or No

Land:

Boat:

Management of belongings:

Garage sale:

Selling online:

Storage? Yes or No
If yes, size and cost:

Planning your route

Weapons for protection:

Mail service:

Important papers:

Will or power of attorney:

Who will you be traveling with?

Significant other

Family or friend

Children

Pets

Last but not least, do you feel emotionally and psychological prepared to travel full time?

If you shouted yes, then you are a warrior!!

84

About the author

Krista Madlung is currently traveling the United States in a Vintage 1967 Bell Trailer with her dog Parley and her two cats, Murray and Sydney. She has started her career as a full time writer after traveling many different career paths within her fully lived life.

Made in the USA
Las Vegas, NV
11 February 2021